MW00526966

Colors Beyond Clouds

A Journey Through the Social Life of a Girl on the Autism Spectrum

Shana Belfast

Abuzz Press

ISBN: 978-1-64438-515-9

Published by Abuzz Press, St. Petersburg, Florida.

Printed on acid-free paper.

This is a work of non-fiction, and it is told entirely from the perspective of the author. The names of all persons have been changed, with the exception of some members of the author's immediate family.

Abuzz Press
2019

First Edition

Library of Congress Cataloging in Publication Data
Belfast, Shana
Colors Beyond Clouds: A Journey Through the Social Life of a Girl on the Autism Spectrum by Shana Belfast
YOUNG ADULT NONFICTION / Biography & Autobiography / General | YOUNG ADULT NONFICTION/ Social Topics / Emotions & Feelings | YOUNG ADULT NONFICTION / Social Topics / Friendship
Library of Congress Control Number: 2019900150

Acknowledgements

So many people helped make this book possible, either by being part of my life and therefore my story, or by helping me with the telling of this story!

I would love to thank my parents, Janine and Shawn Belfast. You are always there for me no matter what I am going through, helping me to be the best version of myself. I love you guys! ☺.

Second, my little brother Julian Belfast. Juju, you are the light of my life! I love you so much! You have a fabulous personality and you are an amazing artist! Thank you for comforting me when I'm upset about school and for helping me feel better. Thank you for sticking up for me and being there for me. I really appreciate having you in my life.

Thanks to everyone in my extended family who supported me throughout my life! Especially Granny Lorns! You all are the best!

My friends (you know who you are!) are very important to me. Thank you for never leaving my side. Thank you for understanding me when I talk about my challenges and for being so supportive. My birthday parties are super fun with all of you. I will always be there for you guys. I love you all.

Thank you to all the wonderful teachers and other school professionals that I have had in middle and high school, who saw something in me and helped me grow. I am especially grateful to my 6th grade teacher Sara Yeterian. She helped me feel comfortable, showed me that she cared, and made me enjoy classes more.

A big thank you to all the music and performing arts teachers and theatre directors that I've had! You taught me about the arts, you believed in me, and pushed me to do my best! I want to shout out my piano teacher…. Debbie Moran! Debbie, you are one of the best teachers that I have had! Thank you so much for teaching me piano, and making it fun! That was my start to loving music!

I am grateful to everyone who took the time to read the manuscript of this book, and who gave me any suggestions or feedback. I am also grateful to Abuzz Press, the publisher of my memoir. I so appreciate it!

Finally, I want to give thanks for my grandfather, George Errol Daisley, who left us to be in heaven before I finished writing this book. Grandpa, thank you for teaching me about faith.

Table of Contents

Prologue

It is early December. The year is 2017. I have waited so long for this. It is time for my first high school musical audition, for *You're a Good Man Charlie Brown*. This is only my fourth audition ever, but I guess I still came a long way.

I practice.
Practice.
Practice.

I am so nervous and excited. The first part of the audition is dance. I'm not great at following choreographies. Following the order of the steps is hard for me. Especially when I need to be in sync with other people.

We had to dance in groups on stage

In front of the other groups.

I danced with a group of kids

To "My New Philosophy."

The steps were not too hard.

I was surprised that I did not have too much trouble. I think that my dance audition actually went well!

I wait...

For the singing auditions. I'm ready for this. I love to sing. My card says #1, which means that I am first to perform. I feel confident and nervous all at the same time.

"Number One", they call.

It's my turn.

I go on stage. I sing "Live Out Loud", a song that I like a lot, from the show *A Little Princess*. It is a good audition song because it is powerful and expressive. The piano starts. I begin to sing. I nail that song.

I'm so proud of my audition!!

I'm so happy!!!!!!!!!!!

For the whole week, I keep checking the theatre program chat site for the results of the audition.

I can't wait for the cast list.

Can't stop thinking about whether I got in or not. Then, a few days later, the show director posts that the list will come out that day. I check the site every few minutes. Nothing yet. But...

Then I see a private message from the show director. It says:

"Hi Shana, unfortunately, you did not make the final list, your audition went well, but we just have a really small cast...."

I am so, so upset.

I have such a passion for theatre.

It could be a whole year until I'm in a show again.

But it's more than just being in a show.

My life was not easy.

I felt alone a lot.

I felt different a lot.

Being on stage helps me forget

Being on stage helps me be part of something more than me

Being on stage helps me cope with difficult feelings.

Theatre has helped me.

But my life is not just theatre

So, my story is not either.

This is my story.

PART ONE: SEARCHING THROUGH THE CLOUDS

Chapter One - This is Me

Hi, my name is Shana. It's pronounced "Shay-na", and I prefer to be called "Shay". I am fourteen years old[1] and a freshman in high school. In addition to singing and theatre, I love unicorns, watching YouTube clips, creating art, listening to Broadway show-tunes, writing poems, and shopping. I live in Westchester County, New York, in a suburb that is about 40 minutes away from midtown Manhattan. I really love that I live so close to New York City, because it is easy to get to my favorite shows. I love New York City even when I am not there to see a show, because I just love the energy of the place, especially Times Square. Times Square is bright and colorful, and has cool shops, like the Disney Store! One evening, I was hanging out in NYC with my family, and after dinner I convinced my parents to drive down to the theatre district, so that I could stage door at the show that my favorite actress

---

[1] I was fourteen when I started this memoir, and turned fifteen just before completing it.

was in. My parents thought that the show had some inappropriate content which was why I wasn't able to see it, but it was so exciting to meet and talk to my inspiration!

I have been writing down my thoughts in journals since I was about 8 years old. I find that writing down what I am thinking about helps me to understand my feelings better. When I was little, I wrote a picture book called *the Princess and the Unicorn*. In it, the princess lost her pet unicorn thanks to an evil fairy. Now, as a teenager, I decided to write this book, to talk about my experiences with having a disorder, and feeling different, and other challenges. The disorder that I have is called autism. I started to write my thoughts about my autism and how it affected me in social, academic, and personal ways after I was having a difficult time. Writing helps me to express my feelings. I also hope that what I say in this book can influence others, or at least let people know that if they are going through something, they are not alone. I want people who read this book to know that going through tough experiences really can make you stronger and not weaker, even if sometimes you do feel weaker.

So first, let's talk about autism. Autism, (or autism spectrum disorder) refers to a wide range of conditions. Some challenges kids with autism have include having trouble connecting socially with other people, repetitive behavior, and/or intense interests. I believe that social problems affected me the most. It was so difficult for me to make friends. As a little kid, even though I spoke pretty normally, I went to speech therapy in my elementary school so that I could practice communicating with other kids. I also went to different social-skills groups outside of school, where the therapist or "teacher" would show the group of kids how to play and what to say in different situations when they were with other kids. I remember going to a social-skills group every week after school in fourth grade, and going into a room and playing with dolls with another girl my age while the therapist looked on and gave us suggestions on what to say.

Social situations are harder for me. I know that I have gone overboard trying to get attention and to make friends. I think that's the reason why a lot of people don't like me, and why my friends sometimes get annoyed with me. For example, I have a good friend now. In middle school, that friend used to say stuff like, "you text too much!" or "you have to stop being such a baby!" It's kind of true that I go overboard and can be a little crazy.... and I also can seem clingy to some people. It's just because when I make new friends, or get added to a group setting or something similar that is social, I feel included, and I get excited, because I spent a lot of my childhood being lonely. The girl who said that is still my friend. I've known her now for four years. I have gotten to know her better and she has gotten to know me. I know now that she says things in a very direct way that can hurt, but she is a good friend. She is funny and we both like singing and hanging out in the mall. My friends now know about my autism.

I believe that autism is the reason why I have such intense interests. When I was little I had an obsession with princesses. I would always talk about princesses, draw them, and wonder about them. In middle school, I became obsessed with the singer Ariana Grande. She always inspired me to keep going with my singing. I was a huge fan, and sometimes felt upset when I thought that I would never meet her or be noticed by her. I used to watch her videos all the time and be sad if my friends were not big fans of hers. I still think she is amazing, listen to her music, and admire her. But in middle school I focused on her a bit too much. I don't have obsessions like that anymore, but I can become too attached to certain people in my life. It bothers me a lot because when you are attached to someone, you think about them too much. When I get attached to people, I get really focused on them, and I don't like that. For example, this is silly, but in 8th grade, I was so attached to my favorite teacher that I got upset because she wrote something on my report card that I didn't like, and I felt that she had betrayed me. She got mad when I tried to speak to her about it and told me that I shouldn't always say what is on my mind and what I feel. It made me feel bad, because I really loved that teacher.

Autism also affects me in school, academically, because I have trouble paying attention. As a young girl with autism, I always felt that I was different. I was a bit embarrassed to have challenges like zoning out in school and the extra classroom support to help me handle those challenges successfully. But now I believe that everyone has challenges that they either have to overcome or deal with. I hope that this book helps not only kids with autism, but anyone who is experiencing a difficult situation where they feel different or uncomfortable.

Colors have always been important to me. This is because I have always loved music, and in my mind, color is very much related to musical sounds. Once as a little girl, I told my mom that a song was very orange. She did not know what I meant, and that was how I found out that the way that I see music as colors is unusual. Later on, I learned that I have a condition called synesthesia, where one of a person's five senses is triggered by another. In my case, when I hear a particular type of sound, it triggers the perception of color in my brain. An estimated 3 to 5 percent of the world population has synesthesia[2], and it is more common in people on the autism spectrum than in the rest of the population. In music, a key is the musical chord that a song revolves around. The song "Somewhere Over the Rainbow" is usually performed in the C-major key. I see this song, and all songs performed in C-major, as warm and yellow. I see some minor keys in dark colors. For example, B minor songs are not warm and happy like C major ones; instead they are dark and mysterious. The song "No Good Deed" from the musical *Wicked* is in B-minor. It is a dark and dramatic blue-purple. The song "Someone Like You" by Adele is performed in A-major. It is a very beautiful song, and like almost all songs in A-major it is either

---

[2] "Synesthesia." *Psychology Today*, Sussex Publishers, www.psychologytoday.com/us/basics/synesthesia.

light red or green, the colors of Christmas. A-major is a lovely, bubbly, but also very relaxing key in music. I also see the individual music notes of songs in different colors. The note G is dark orange. The note D is red.

In addition to music, I see numbers, months of the year, and days of the week in color. Most odd numbers are shades of either pink or blue, but the number 1 has no color. Even numbers are 'hot' colors. For example, 6 is orange. I see the days of the week in my head inside a rectangle filled with colored boxes. Each day is in a box of a different color. Monday is pink. Wednesday is green. Friday is purple. I do not believe that having synesthesia has affected me either positively or negatively, but it is a part of who I am and how I think.

I live with my dad, mom, and brother, Julian who is three and a half years younger than me. I love my family so much. They are very supportive of me in everything, and I'm super grateful for that. My family always supports me by going to my shows, and taking me places. We also do fun things together. On summer vacation, we go on road trips and vacations together. We especially love beach vacations. One of the best vacations that I've been on with my family was a trip to Trinidad, which is the country that my parents are from. We spent a month there, and it was so warm, and there were lots of beaches. In Trinidad, we stayed at my grandparents' home, a beautiful pink house surrounded by palm trees. We also went to the neighboring island of Tobago with cousins and took a boat out to the Nylon Pool, which is a natural shallow pool in the middle of the deep ocean. There, we swam in the warm, crystal clear water and admired the schools of brightly colored fish that shared the pool with us. That was a wonderful vacation, and it was great to bond with my family. We have a lot of fun.

My little brother, Julian is super-cool, and I think that having a brother makes me more social. My relationship with Julian is not always the best. He takes my iPhone to watch videos and play games, and then I get mad, because he has his own phone! I know that it is because our parents restrict his online access, but it still makes me mad. He spends way too much time videogaming with his friends. One game in particular that he loves is called Roblox. Actually, according to Julian it's not a game, it's a "gaming social media platform". He asks me to play Roblox with him, but I don't play often. I would like to do other things with him, like painting or even playing a game outside. He gets really upset with me for this, and tells me that he hates me. I sometimes feel bad about our relationship, but most of the siblings that I know of fight so maybe it is not so bad. And maybe our relationship will be better when we are older! I call him "Chubby Cheeks". He doesn't really like when I call him that, but it's a bit addicting because he is cute. I feel like he taught me how to fight and stand up for myself in a fun way. And I believe that we do care a lot for each other even if we do fight. I love to go to his soccer games to support him, even though I find soccer really boring. And whenever I scream because I see a spider or some other insect, Julian will run to find me, and get that bug away from me. Oops. I just remembered. Last time this happened, he caught the bug and then chased me down to put it on me, so never mind. But he is really a good kid. Sometimes I let him hide out in my room when he is not supposed to be online and we watch YouTube videos together.

My mom and dad are very supportive of me and I love them, but there are many things that I wish they would understand. I wish that my parents, (and many other people) would be more understanding of my feelings and autism. For example, my mom sometimes thinks that I put people on a pedestal too much. I know that she gets annoyed about it. I told her that it was hard to control getting attached to people, and she said that I could control it and not to use having autism as an excuse. But I do believe that my autism causes this, since it makes my brain over-focus sometimes. It is hard getting so attached to people, because of the repetitive thoughts and anxiety that I experience. I wish my mom would understand that. But I know that my mom is tough on me for things like this because she loves me and does not want me to keep getting hurt. Even though she can be tough, I know I can go to her to talk about anything.

I also wish that both of my parents would understand more about how it feels to be left out. In middle school, I used to get in trouble with them for the way I used texting to reach out to make friends, since they used to monitor my phone. For example, one time my dad got upset with me for texting someone that I wanted an invitation to an event that I wasn't invited to. It stressed me out when they got angry like that, because I felt that they didn't know what I was really going through, and what it was like to be left out of everything. They are always behind me though, and are smart and fun, so I am thankful to have them!

My faith in God is also very important to me as a Christian, and it is an important part of how I handle my challenges. If things aren't going well for me, I say a prayer to God, my Lord and Savior. I have a lot of confidence that He will set me on the right path in life. Even when things are going well, I send a prayer to Him, thanking Him for what He has done for me in my life.

Chapter Two - My Social History

My autism was discovered in the early years of my life. I honestly don't really remember my early years, so I can't write that much about those times, and most of what I am writing about before I was four years old was what my mom told me when I asked her about it. She said that I did not speak much. When I was two years old, my parents took me to a preschool to socialize with other kids. At the preschool, I kept knocking things down from tables for no reason, which was unusual for a two-year-old. I moved around the classroom constantly, was in my own world, and never tried to connect with the other kids. One day after the class, the teacher told my mom that I had a "situation" because of the knocking things down, and thought that I might have a special need. After that, from ages two to five, I went to three different pre-schools that helped kids who had challenges like I did. At all the schools, my mom and my teachers in the preschool had a special way of communicating. They used a notebook. My teachers would write about how I was behaving in the class every day in the notebook. My mom sometimes wrote back to the teacher in the notebook. My mom showed me all of the notebooks that she kept from those early days and I learned a lot about myself when I was younger from reading them. One of the things the teachers wrote about the most was that I had trouble eating. I was a very picky eater, and still am! As a preschooler I liked sweets, crunchy foods, cheese and hot dogs. But not much else. I also sometimes didn't eat lunch and threw it all over the floor. One time, I even tried to steal another kid's lunch because it looked better than my own. I also learned from those notebooks that I used to ask questions that I already knew the answer to. I remember doing that, even later on when I was older. In kindergarten I asked the other kids what their favorite color was, pretty much every day. I just felt happier and more comfortable when I heard them say what I knew they were going to say! Sometimes I still have the impulse to ask questions that I know the answer to, but I can control it.

My experiences in elementary school, especially from second grade to fifth grade are the experiences that have affected me the most. I remember always feeling like I was different and believing that everyone in my grade hated me. I almost always felt left out. And I would try to explain to kids sometimes that I was sad because they did not want to play with me, but they never understood. They got mad at me for interrupting them. In my opinion, most people just don't understand how this feels.

I don't remember my kindergarten years too much. What I remember most about first grade is that I was very impulsive and silly, to the point where I was out of control. It was very hard for me to sit still. I had this constant urge to move, and sitting still felt very uncomfortable. I spent a lot of the time in class playing around with this wild and crazy boy. We were both wild and crazy. We used to chase each other around the class while the class was in session, and the teachers would yell at us. I had a homeroom teacher and a language arts teacher. One day my language arts teacher screamed at me, "I am going to kick you out of my class!" I was so terrified because I thought she would use her foot to kick me out the door. I was also really embarrassed.

My first-grade experience honestly didn't have a huge impact on me, but the other years in elementary school did. Second grade was the worst. The beginning was fine. I did not run around anymore. I could sit still for longer. I had a friend to play with. I really liked her, and depended on her, because she was the only person I played with at recess. We would do everything together. But a few weeks into second grade, she found another best friend. I tried to play with them, but they excluded me. One time, they said that I broke one of their purses, and were very mean about it. I had no one to play with and was very lonely. Social situations were so hard - I just did not know how to make friends. Every day, at recess in second grade, I would cry on the floor all by myself because I felt that no one wanted me. Some people teased me for it. Everyone stayed away from me. I remember once a kid telling an older kid in another grade something like, "Shana cries only because she has no one to play with." The older kid laughed and said how stupid I was. There was also this really mean girl who would tease and bully me. I'm going to call her Danielle (not her real name). Whenever I tried to speak, Danielle would tell me that no one cared about what I had to say. She would also imitate me crying and make fun of me. The year was so tough. Everyone hated me. This is silly, but one time I felt so lonely that I raised my hand in class and said that I had no friends. I wasn't invited to any birthday parties. My mom would give me suggestions on making friends and keeping relationships, but they were hard to follow.

Third grade was not so good either. My teacher was a shouter, did not understand me and made me feel very anxious. For example, in class I would sometimes quietly read aloud because at that time I understood better when reading out loud, and she would yell at me and tell the kid next to me "Lisa, just tell me if Shana bothers you". The kids were not nicer, either. I would try to talk to kids and they would get annoyed. I tried to make new friends. One time, I heard girls talking about a dog and I asked a question about what they were talking about. One girl asked why I always butt into people's conversations. Another girl said that it was none of my business. In third grade, I had a play-date with a girl who I'm actually friends with now. She was very nice and we had a lot in common, but a little after the play-date, she stopped talking to me and started being really rude. I'm not sure why. Other kids were just completely cruel, and did not sugar-coat their feelings. One girl said directly to my face at recess, "We do not want to play with you." I guess I understand why a lot of people didn't like me. I was a lonely, weird annoying little girl. Another time, two girls talked to me in private and told me that they didn't want me to annoy them. Then sometime later one of those two girls,

I'll call her Chrissy, complained during recess about this girl who always begged her for food. Someone else asked if that annoying girl was me. It actually wasn't me but being known for being annoying hurt.

There were also moments outside of school, like at summer camp, where kids treated me badly. I used to ask a lot of questions, and said and did things without thinking. One day, at girl scout camp, I was with a group of girls in a tent house. One girl was talking about how an alligator once bit her through her stomach, and I didn't really understand, and was very curious about it. I kept on asking her questions about it, and she and the other girls got really mad at me. I remember someone saying, "You just don't get it!" There were many occasions where campers got angry with me. One time, at another camp I was being very repetitive. It was in an art class. I kept saying "I'm a fairy princess." I knew it was annoying to keep saying it over and over again, but I just wanted someone to respond to what I was saying. Then some girl said, "We get it

Shana, you're a fairy princess." At the same camp, there was a tiny girl who I think had a disability. She was in our age group but looked like a preschooler, and was very thin. I would try to pick her up because she was so small. Some girl told me that I annoyed the small girl. I didn't really understand at the time that it wasn't a good thing to act like that. At camp I tried to hang out with kids, but just like in school, they would get annoyed. It really wasn't just school where I felt like everywhere I went, kids were against me.

Moving on back to school, I actually don't really know how to describe fourth grade, but it wasn't the best. The good part was that I was in a "gymnastics club" at recess, started by two girls, one a fifth grader and the other in my grade. I was the only other member of the club, other than those two girls. Every day, we would meet outside on the yellow, green, and blue playground at the back of the school. The girls taught me to do kick-overs, handstands, splits, and backbends. The two girls who ran the club sort of bossed me around, telling me what to do. If I did not listen to them or if they thought that I was not paying attention, for punishment they would move me down to the previous, lower level that I had been on. I would have to work harder to get back to the higher level. Even so, I enjoyed it. I had discovered something that I loved. Gymnastics was the first activity that I became passionate about. It was really fun, and for the rest of fourth and fifth grade, I would do gymnastics, because it made me happy, even though I was lonely. Gymnastics made me feel powerful. Eventually I got my parents to sign me up for classes at a gymnastics place for after school.

I was not happy when I lost one of the girls from the school gymnastics club as a friend. She was the fifth grader, so she was older than I was. She pushed me (a little too hard) to do well in the club and at gymnastics. We had a couple of playdates. Once I got to know her she was kind and fun. When I moved up to fifth grade and she moved on to middle school, I would see her sometimes after school when she came to pick up her younger siblings. I missed her a lot. But she had moved on. I did gymnastics moves on the playground after school hoping that she would join in so that it would be how it used to be, but she did not. Instead she would talk to other middle school kids who were at the elementary school meeting their siblings like her. One time, I cried because she ignored me, and she talked to me about it. She told me that I should try to make new friends. After that, she stopped talking to me and it made me sad. I realized eventually that she wasn't a great friend after all, because when I thought about it, our relationship was mostly about her showing me how to improve my gymnastics moves and nothing else.

Elementary school was not a good experience for me, but I'm glad that it introduced me to gymnastics, something that I loved. When fifth grade was over I was excited for middle school.

My "tween" years or middle school years were better because I had more opportunities to connect with other kids. I was not amazing at social situations, and felt awkward a lot, but I did meet kids who became friends. I also lost friends. I was very aware of my autism in my tween years, and had low self-confidence. I was very nervous but excited for middle school. Sixth grade turned out to be a good year academically. I got high honor roll for 3 marking periods, and honor roll for the 4th marking period. The 4th marking period was harder because I broke my arm in the spring at gymnastics class and had to do surgery, but I still did well. I had a co-teacher in 6th grade, because my IEP said that I needed one. The IEP or Individual Education Plan is a document that kids with special needs have that spells out what sort of help they need from the school to function well in class. Because of autism, I can lose focus in class and get very distracted, so my teachers thought that to do my best I needed a class with a co-teacher, that is, a class with an extra teacher. Most of the kids in the class were "typical" and did not need the extra teacher. The co-teacher was very sweet, but she tried to help me with a lot of things. She would try to write my homework down for me at times when I wanted to be more independent. She was a very sweet lady, and one of the best teachers I have ever had, but getting help was so embarrassing. By 6th grade, I knew a ton about my autism and challenges, because I read many books about people with autism. I was so conscious of needing the extra help. At times, when the co-teacher tried to help me, I wouldn't let her. I was afraid people would see her help me and think I was dumb or a "baby". Having the extra support made me feel not normal.

One time, in science in sixth grade we were learning about nervous system disorders. We had to pick three disorders to talk about, and autism was one of them. I felt really ashamed and did not want to pick it. I hated that it was a choice. But eventually, I picked autism because my mom encouraged me to. She told me that it was good to learn about it, and now I agree.

Having the extra support was particularly difficult because I wanted to be socially accepted. I wanted to be friends with a really pretty and popular girl, but I'm sure that she thought I was weird. One day, I was testing with the co-teacher. Sometimes I do tests away from the rest of the class, and just with a teacher, to avoid distractions, and this was one such time. The co-teacher asked the popular girl to tell our teacher for the next period that I was working with her and I would be late for class. She gave the girl a note to give to the other teacher. I'm pretty sure that after that, the girl thought I was special-ed, and didn't want to be my friend.

In 6th grade, I got social media, and I think that also lowered my self-esteem. I didn't really know how to use it, so I posted really weird and crazy things. People talked about me. One time I posted a crazy video of me dancing, and people told me a year after I posted the video that others talked bad about me. Of course, I deleted all the crazy posts, but I still use Instagram and like it. I know that it is not good for my self-esteem, but it's fun. Other than the challenges, 6th grade was cool. I made a couple of friends and the extra-curricular activities and the school work was more interesting that at elementary school.

Seventh grade wasn't so good. At the end of sixth grade, I had begged my parents to take me out of the co-taught classroom setting for the next school year. One reason was that I had gotten high enough grades in sixth to do advanced math and science classes in seventh grade, and advanced classes did not have co-teachers. But the real reason that I wanted to not be in the co-taught class was that I wanted to stop feeling "special ed". My parents and teachers listened, so for seventh grade I had no co-teacher, and was in advanced math and science. I also started a foreign language, so I had one additional class. It was a very stressful year. My grades dropped, bigtime. It wasn't really that the work was that much harder. It was more that there was just so much to keep track of. And I did not have a co-teacher to remind me to write down homework or to check to make sure I had all my notes. I kept losing my homework. I zoned out a lot in class and sometimes did not keep up.

Seventh grade taught me that it was important to do what was right for me. I had encouraged my parents at the end of 6th grade to ask for a classroom setting that did not require me to have extra support, so that I would not be seen as a special-ed kid. But because of that decision, my grades dropped. Although I really did not want to be in a co-taught class again, by the end of 7th grade I realized that I needed it. I learned that it is very important to get the help you need to achieve your goals, even if it does not make you feel good sometimes.

Seventh grade was a bit crazy socially. I became friends with a group of girls, which was pretty cool, but that didn't mean that everything was "perfect". For recess, we hung out on the black-top outside. Sometimes even when I was with them, I felt that I was being left out. I would either be super quiet in that group, or be loud and sort of inappropriate just to be noticed. I think that this bothered some of the girls. I learned that the group wasn't right for me, because their interests were different. They always talked about Anime, which I was not interested in, or gross stuff like sexual situations in movies, which I also was not interested in. Sometimes I would act silly just to fit in with them. I knew that I was not being myself. So even though I was part of a group, it didn't feel right to me.

In seventh grade, I got bullied. I had this non-graded class called "tech-ed" that I didn't like at all. I honestly don't even remember how the bullying started, but in that class I had to sit next to some boys who spent the whole period making jokes and laughing. Then they started talking about me. They would say stupid things about my body. At first I would laugh along with them just to show that I did not care about what they were saying. But then it did not stop. It happened every day and I got a little bit tired of it. I told my mom, especially about the boy who kept talking about my body. She emailed the teacher about the kids harassing me. The next day, I went into that class, and the teacher called me into another room. The boys and two girls who normally sat near to me were assembled there. The teacher had already questioned the boys, as well as the two girls who had heard what was going on in the class. Both the boys and the two girls laughed at me when I came in. The teacher made the boy who was most responsible apologize to me. It made me upset to see those kids laughing at me. The boys' harassing me was annoying, but it did not upset me the way that the girls laughing at me did. It crushed me to think that the girls hated me. One of them was very pretty and I would have liked to be her friend. She had long, black, curly hair. One time afterwards I accidently touched her hair or something like that, and she said "uggh, Shana." She always laughed at me when others were being mean. It took a while, but I figured out eventually that she wasn't someone that I should want to be friends with. She was pretty, but that didn't mean that she was a great person. I realized then that for some reason, growing up I always thought that people who were prettier were nicer than other people. I do not know why I assumed this. But my experience in 7th grade with this girl taught me that being nice has nothing to do with being pretty. Niceness is about choosing to treat people the way that you want to be treated. People of all different looks, sizes, shapes and colors can make or not make that choice.

For eighth grade my parents and teachers decided that we needed to make changes to my classroom setting so that I could have a better year academically. I went back to being in a co-taught class like in sixth. Additionally, for the last period every day I was in a class called resource room, where a small number of kids got extra help with classwork for every subject. Resource room was good for me because I got to review the work I did in class that day with the teacher with only about four or five other kids there. I also got a head start on my homework. My grades improved. However, there were a couple of boys in my tech-ed class who knew I was going to resource room and called me "Ed" (short for special education) and "dumb". Most of the bad stuff seemed to happen in tech-ed class. Maybe since it was not a regular academic class where kids got a letter grade, some students thought that it was ok to behave badly. Being in resource room and being in a co-taught class again brought back the feelings of embarrassment and self-consciousness that I had in sixth grade about having autism. But what was different about eighth grade was that I realized how much I missed getting good grades and doing well academically. I needed to have these supports even if they made me feel uncomfortable, to accomplish my eighth-grade academic goals, and to be successful despite my challenges.

Even so, eighth grade was a good year. I made friends. I am still close to some of them now. I also met people who I became friends with but who eventually turned out to be not that great. I met Chloe (not her real name) at the end of seventh grade. We had eighth grade science together, and we got to be close. She was really fun. We'd sit next to each other in class and she would make jokes about the teachers that would crack me up. She also helped me one time when a teacher constantly gave me a hard time about my disorganized binder. She told me that he was not treating me properly and kept encouraging me to talk to another teacher about it. She gave me good advice. She really liked me, and we did everything together. I guess I would say that I depended on her a lot, to help me and to tell me what to do. I was excited that someone was really into me. I don't feel like people are that into me often, and she called me her best friend, which made me very happy. Over the summer, which was the summer before high school, we hung out at video game arcades and amusement parks. Although I liked hanging out with her, she sometimes said and did things that troubled me. She took money that my mom gave me when we went to the amusement park, saying that she would keep it safe. She wanted to decide what rides we would go on or what games we'd play. She had a boyfriend and sometimes when he came she told me that she wanted to be alone with him on rides. But she was still my friend and I was happy that we were together in most classes when high school started.

In high school, Chloe excluded me from things. One day when it was close to Halloween, she told me that she got invited to another friend, Tina's, Halloween party. After school a few days later, Chloe skyped me and said that she wished that I could come to the party, but that I was not invited. She told me that Tina's mom only allowed 6 or 7 kids. I had forgotten about Tina's party and I told Chloe that I understood. She kept bringing that party up and about how excited she was in conversation all the time. One day at lunch I sat in the cafeteria with Chloe and one of our other friends, a boy named Anthony (not his real name). Chloe kept talking about hanging out for Halloween, and would sometimes whisper things in Anthony's ear. I heard her whisper "Yes, Tina said that you can come to her house". I felt really hurt, by both Chloe and Tina. I had invited Tina to my birthday party earlier in the year. But I understood that she could not invite everyone. I was more disappointed about how Chloe kept talking nonstop to me about the party that I wasn't invited to. I hated that she decided to invite Anthony to Tina's party, whispering loudly right in front of me while I was sitting with them at the table. Another time, Chloe and I were walking in the hallway in high school. Chloe told me that she was going to a popular fast food place near the school later that day. She told me "you're not going", which I thought was very rude of her. She got mad at me for little things and bossed me around. One time, she even told me that I should be in special-ed classes, because of my zoning out in class. She felt that she knew all the time what was best for me. A couple of times I told her that she was being mean, and she would apologize and say that she was going through a hard time because of her parents' divorce. But she would go right back to being mean. It took a very long time to realize that she was a bad friend, but I cut her out. I think that was a good idea, because of how she treated me. I'm sure that she was mean because I let her have power over me whenever I made it seem like she was "better" or "older" that me. My experience with her taught me to not let people boss me around as much. It also made me realize that I had to stand up for myself more.

Chapter Three – Communication, Conversation and Confusion

Making friends is so important to me, but connecting with other kids to start and keep friendships is hard. One of the worst mistakes I made began over the summer before high school started, and continued through the first part of freshman year. I tried hard to be friends with a group of girls who I knew from middle school. I was about to turn fourteen. I talked to one of my friends, named Urleen about how it would be really nice to be part of a girl squad. She told me to ask a girl named Becky, who was part of a group, to add me to a chat with them. On my birthday, I texted Becky with the request to add me to her group-chat with her squad. She said she would make a new chat with her friends, including me. She made it. I let the group know that it was my birthday. Most of them wished me happy birthday. Over the next few weeks of the summer, I texted the group. Sometimes they wouldn't respond, and they didn't ask me to hang out with them or anything. I invited them to the musical theatre show that I was in. I really wanted them to come to see me perform. When I texted them about that show the first time, some of them responded. Two of them couldn't go but wished me luck, and some of them said they would see if they could come. Then, when the time came closer to the show I told them again and no one responded. I felt really hurt. I even told them that I felt hurt and only two people responded.

Then one day in the fall after school started, I sat at lunch with another girl from that group chat called Annie (not her real name). I saw that she had a chat going with the same group of girls that I communicated with over the summer. I know now that this wasn't the smartest thing to do, but I added myself to the chat on her phone. I was really excited because I thought this was another chance to be part of the group. At some point, they had stopped texting in the chat that was formed on my birthday. I felt really bad because they didn't include me in their hangouts, so I texted them about it. I said that I felt they were doing things without me and that I did not like that they excluded me. One girl texted, "Sorry you feel that way but everyone hangs out with different people and you're not going to be included in everything." Another girl said, "You can't expect to be included just because you're in a group chat." I wasn't expecting to be included in every single hang out, but it hurt that they seemed not to like me and didn't include me in anything. I even asked them if they wanted to hang out for Halloween, and they said that they were not sure what they were doing. I saw later from social media that every single person in the chat hung out on the Friday before Halloween, and some of them got together the day of Halloween. I know that they didn't really know me too well, but I felt like they were not trying to get to know me, and that they hated me. Even though I was going a bit "overboard" at times, I was friendly towards those girls. I was really confused, sad, and hurt. I knew one of the girls in the chat, Cathy, better than the others. I asked her why the girls didn't like me, and the first and second time I asked she didn't really respond to me. I asked her a third time, and she told me the truth. She said she didn't want to hurt my feelings, but that some people didn't feel comfortable with me. They didn't like that I added myself to the group chat with them that day when I was in the school cafeteria. I was a little confused, because I was in a chat with them before, the very first chat that Becky had created. It wasn't the best idea to add myself, but I really wanted to be in the group. Cathy is still a friend and is really kind, but back then it seemed that she didn't know how difficult it was for me to connect with other people.

I decided to tell Cathy and the group about my autism, because I thought it would be a good idea to have them understand me more. When I told them, they said that I didn't have to apologize for anything, which made me mad, because I knew I bothered them. This experience was very difficult, but it also helped me understand that it does not make sense to try to force friendships. This was not the only occasion where I had problems with kids not understanding me.

A girl told me that I gave her a panic attack once, which made me wonder what I did to upset people. There was also a girl in my vocal performing arts class who didn't like me and excluded me a lot. Whenever I talked she acted annoyed. I texted her to ask her about it, and her response made me want to have a breakdown. She said that when I tried to talk to her and her friends, I always talked about my autism and it was really annoying. She also said that I tried to get attention by crying all the time. I cried when I saw her text. To make things worse, I was in a performance that day and I couldn't stop thinking about what she said.

I cared a lot about what other people thought of me, and had anxiety about it. This really started in middle school, but it became bigger in high school. One day in the cafeteria during lunch period, I did something that wasn't a great idea. I picked up the phone of one of my friends and searched for my name in her text messages, to see what people were saying about me. I didn't get to see much of the things that were said, but the friend got uncomfortable that I was looking at her messages and told me to give back her phone. Eventually, I gave her back, and I felt bad because it was wrong to look at her messages like that, but I really wanted to know why so many people were against me.

There was another situation with one of my other friends that happened the summer after my first year of high school. My friend's name was Judy. Judy and I were in the school play together back in eighth grade when we were still at middle school. She hated the play's director, and we would always talk about that, and about another teacher who gave me trouble. She was very sweet and outgoing. I did not like that sometimes at lunch she sat with people who made fun of me, and laughed along when they teased me. I talked to her about it, and she was completely understanding, and kind, and apologized to me. High school came, and we were still friends. I was in the vocal performing arts program, and she was in the acting program. She made a lot of new friends from her acting class, and I felt that she preferred to be with them more than me. I made new friends also, but I still made the time to talk to her. I was friendly with her, but she changed. When I sat with her at lunch, she talked with the other friends she made. I just felt that Judy had no time for me. I realized that it could have been because I was going through a hard time in high school, and spent too much time telling her about my problems. I texted Judy that I felt that she was ignoring me, and I apologized for anything I may have done wrong. She was nice about it. I know now that I went too far with telling her how I felt. When the school year ended and summer started, we made plans to hang out when I got back from sleepaway camp. When I returned from sleepaway I texted her asking what she was doing for the rest of summer, and she said she was taking a musical theatre class. She told me that she couldn't hang out, because she was busy with the class, and with summer homework. I understood, but felt upset. She had been very enthusiastic about hanging out with me at the beginning of summer. I texted her about getting together a few more times, and each time she said, "maybe, I'll see" but nothing happened. So I texted her about being disappointed because we had promised to get together and that she was breaking the promise. She wrote a response that really hurt my feelings. Judy told me that I couldn't keep writing paragraphs about how I felt she didn't like me. I understood why she got annoyed with it, but I explained to her that she wasn't being a very nice friend. I told her that I was being a good friend and made time for her, and she didn't make time for me. She told me that she made lots of new friends that she was closer with. She said that we were not that close anymore. Judy was also harsh and told me to "actually stop writing paragraphs." Her text made me cry. It especially hurt when she told me that we were not close. I had so many good memories with her. Judy was, and is a nice person. Eventually I felt that the situation wasn't about who was right or wrong, it maybe was about how we had different perspectives on the relationship. While I felt that Judy was not being a good friend, maybe she felt that she was trying but didn't want to be that close. I have no idea what our relationship will be like in the future but I learned that it is sometimes okay to let friends go. Judy was, and still is a good person, but maybe I was looking for too much in a friend, or maybe she was not the right friend for me. She could have been a better friend to another person, but a "casual" friend to me. Next time I will try not to push so hard.

Some of my friends were really kind and understanding when I explained my autism situation to them. I was so happy when this happened. In my first year of high school, at the beginning of the year, I met this girl, who I will call Yazmin. We are still good friends. She thought that I was shy at first and asked me why I never talked to anyone. I get really anxious in many social situations, and sometimes I don't speak to anyone because I don't want to seem like I am trying too hard to make friends, or seem too awkward or anything. I decided to text that girl to tell her about my autism. She texted me back that it was fine and not to define myself by a disorder. She also said that there was nothing wrong with being autistic, and that my disorder wasn't the problem, it was society that was the problem. She helped me feel better about myself, and I agreed with her. I really do feel like society views autism in a negative way. Some people even use the term as an insult. Having autism shouldn't be looked at as a bad thing, or be stereotyped. There are many successful people who have autism, and who overcame challenges. For some of them, like animal behavior expert Temple Grandin, autism was helpful even. Differences aren't automatically a bad thing.

I thought it was important to tell another person about my autism. Allie was a girl who was super-talented. She had a great voice and she had leads in all the middle school and high school plays. I kept trying to be her friend, even though I knew I may be annoying her with frequent texts. I honestly didn't want her to not like me, because she was really cool and sweet. So, I texted her about my autism and she told me it was fine and that she understood. She also said that she thought I was still one of the sweetest and most caring people that she knew, and that she enjoyed my persona and presence. I was very surprised that she said she thought that I didn't need to explain myself. I definitely needed to explain, but her kind words made me happy. Many of my other friends said really nice things, that my autism diagnosis made no difference to them, and that they still thought that I was an amazing person. I really liked that. I was so nervous to tell people about my autism at first, but I am glad that I did.

PART TWO: DISCOVERING MY COLORS

Chapter Four - Disappointments and Bouncing Back

So, that's pretty much been the story of my life. It has been rocky but guess what? There have been so many good times, and I have learned so much. Remember me back in December of my high school freshman year? I had just suffered the WORST rejection – I did not get picked for the high school theatrical production of *You're a Good Man Charlie Brown*. I cried and cried and cried. Then I stopped crying and remembered that there were places that put on productions outside of high school. I had even been in a theatrical production at a place like that the summer before. I searched the internet for theatres not too far from where I lived, that put on shows with school aged casts. And guess what? I FOUND ONE in a neighboring town that was putting on a new show with auditions in the next few weeks! I went to the audition. I sang the same song that I did for the high school audition. There was no dance part, but I had to read from a script in front of the audition panel. I thought it went well. But after the last time, I was not sure what would happen. A week later, the results were out and I got an amazing role, which included a singing solo as well as a pretty major acting part. It was for a musical called *25th Annual Putnam County Spelling Bee*. I learned from this experience that it is better to look at more than one solution when you are trying to accomplish any goal. That way, you are not as disappointed if one option does not work out, because there are others that you may be able to fall back on.

Practicing for the show was not easy. I had to do my homework before going to rehearsals 3 or 4 times a week. Not to mention..in the middle of the month of rehearsals leading up to the show, I got the biggest SHOCK that completely changed my LIFE!

Chapter Five - Shocks
and New Normals

I went on vacation with my family for winter break, which started soon after I got the part in the *25th Annual Putnam County Spelling Bee* production. We had a great time in New Orleans, but everyone in my family kept asking me why I was drinking so much water, and why I was going to the bathroom all the time! My parents even told me to stop drinking so much, especially when we were about to board a plane, but I just could not help myself. When we returned home, I went back to school, and to rehearsing for the play after school. I was very busy, juggling homework, studying for tests, rehearsing for the show, and weekend commitments (I belonged to an afterschool club that performed for senior citizens at nursing homes). I still felt thirsty all the time, but life went on as usual. Then, one morning about a week after we were back from vacation, I woke up with a pain in my abdominal area. My mom took me to the doctor. The doctor made me give her a urine sample. Then she ordered blood tests. Then she told my mom that I had to go straight to the Emergency Room of the nearby hospital because I had very high blood sugar! This could have been extremely dangerous. At the hospital, I was diagnosed with type 1 diabetes, also called juvenile diabetes. The nurse explained what type 1 diabetes was. Type 1 diabetes happens when not enough (or no) insulin is being made by the organ called the pancreas. Insulin is needed to move the glucose sugar created when food is digested to all the cells of the body. In type 1 diabetes, your body becomes allergic to some of the cells in your pancreas, and your immune system tries to destroy your own pancreas, so that your ability to make insulin is reduced. This happens because of genetics and not because of any diet or exercise habits. I was very worried, and missed days of school, because I was in the hospital. The doctors and nurses showed me how to check my blood sugar and how to inject insulin. It was pretty scary, and painful at first, because I have always been afraid of needles. Now I had to prick myself to test my sugar AND inject myself with insulin after every meal and snack! Everything was really different, and I felt like my life was going to change.

I was so upset. Once again, something happened to me that made me different from everyone else. Autism has been a big challenge, but this was different. I had my whole life to learn about how to "be on the autism spectrum" and survive. With diabetes, I had to stay in the hospital and learn from the nurses and doctors how to do insulin shots, because they said I could not leave until my parents and I knew how to take care of the diabetes. If I didn't take care of it now, I could get very sick.

After a few days in "diabetes training" at the hospital I realized that both having autism and adapting to having autism has helped me to get used to diabetes.

I tested my sugar and injected insulin 6 times a day, sometimes more. I was always "on top of my game" in terms of remembering when it was time, and even pointed out when my parents made a mistake. This became like a routine to me quickly, compared to my mom and dad. My mind likes to have a routine. Step by step ways of doing things feel normal. From what I have read, other people with autism feel the same way. But also, I made learning how to go through the steps a priority because it was about my health so it was important to me.

On the day before I left, the doctor took me, my parents and another family whose son had also just been diagnosed with diabetes into a room to review everything that we needed to do when we went home and to "test" us. He said he would not let us leave the hospital unless we passed the test! The doctor started asking questions about how to handle situations, really fast, to me and the boy. "What do you do if you test and your blood sugar is less than 70?" "What do you have to do before you go to gym at school?" "What are the symptoms of low blood sugar that you need to look out for?" He was asking the questions one after the other, pausing for just a few seconds between questions for us to answer. The other kid answered. I knew the answers but it took more time for me to figure out what he said, so when I started to answer he was asking the next question. At one point, I interrupted him, and asked him to go slower when asking the questions. I had learned how to "self-advocate" over the years. Self-advocating just means speaking up for yourself to tell teachers and other people what you need. At school, because I take a little longer to process information, and because I understand concepts better when they are broken down into steps, speaking up to teachers has become something that I need to do if I want to do well in school. Self-advocating is easy at home because I know my parents and I know that they want me to speak up when I want something. But it can be difficult in school and other places outside of my family life, because it means that you have to interrupt the teacher or other adult who is in charge, and they might not have a great reaction to you. For example, one time in class my teacher realized that I did not finish something, and she got really angry. I did not finish it because that day I had a hard time concentrating on my work though I tried hard. I should have explained to her that I was feeling very unfocused and needed more time to complete the assignment. But I was too nervous to tell her. I am glad that most of the time now I can get over feeling a little scared about talking to an adult so that I can get what I need. At the hospital, once I told the doctor, he slowed down and I answered his questions. So I got to leave the hospital the next day!

Having diabetes is another thing that makes me stand out, but I would say that I adapted to it pretty quickly. Getting used to diabetes was quick, but it was also difficult. For the first month, I had to stick myself to get blood to test for my glucose level before every meal and every snack, and also late at night. But that was not the worst part. The worst part was that once I got tested for blood sugar levels before eating, and then estimated the grams of carbohydrates that I would be eating, I had to use an insulin pen to inject myself with the correct amount of insulin. And then at night, I injected myself with a special, longer lasting type of insulin. That needle was worse than the others. In all I had to inject myself with an insulin needle six times a day, plus do finger sticks each time to get blood to test to find out sugar levels. It was not easy, but I got used to it because I had to. Sometimes I cried for the night-time insulin shot though.

After I was diagnosed, I felt really alone at school. Every day I had to leave my choral class early to go to the nurse because that was the class that I had right before lunch. I had to do the testing and injections at the nurse's office. It was really embarrassing at first, but I got used to it. It was also stressful because I had to eat lunch in the cafeteria within 15 minutes of taking insulin in the nurse's office which was far from the cafeteria. It was a rush.

About a month after I was diagnosed, in April of my high school freshman year, I got fitted with a fabulous device called an Omnipod, which is a pump that releases insulin into my body as needed, so that I no longer needed to do insulin injections! I just use a hand-held device called a PDM, or Personal Diabetes Manager, to enter how many grams of carbohydrates I was about to eat, and the PDM would wirelessly tell the pod how much insulin to give me! The pod is a disposable device that needs to be changed every three days, and there is slight discomfort when it is changed sometimes, but nowhere near the pain of the insulin pen injections that I had to do previously! This made my life so much easier! Later on in the year, I will get another amazing device called a continuous glucose monitor, which will replace the finger sticks I need to do to get the blood to test for my blood sugar level. I would just be able to stick it on my body and read the blood sugar number off of another wireless device! I cannot wait.

My dad helped me so much with getting used to diabetes. When I was on the insulin injections, he gave me the shots at first because I was too scared to do it myself. He also convinced me that I could do it on my own, and showed me the best places on my body to give myself shots. My dad, who is an engineer, was really great at finding the latest and greatest solutions in diabetes technology, and he got me on the right devices that would make the situation as painless as possible. Even when I moved on to the Omnipod pump he would pinch my skin so that when the tiny needle on the disposable pod went in I would not feel a thing. He can be a bit strict about things, but he still considers how I feel when making hard decisions. I am very thankful for his support and involvement. He did a lot for me during this difficult time, and he still does, and I love him! Thank you, Dad! (If and when you read this).

Around March, when I was diagnosed with diabetes, I started thinking about summer. I love summer partly because my birthday is in the summer and I was looking forward to turning fifteen. But also, this summer I really wanted to go to a sleep-away camp. It seemed like a lot of fun. Many of the kids I went to school with went back to the same camp every year, and kept posting on social media about how it was such a great experience. I wanted a camp with all girls, so I searched and searched on the internet for one. I saw a few camps that I wanted to go to, but my parents were considering a camp for kids with diabetes, because I had just gotten diagnosed. Later, we agreed that the camp for kids with diabetes would be better. I really wanted to go to one of the other camps, but I was still pretty excited. Finally, summer came. I started packing towels, cute bathing suits, pillows, clothes and more! I was super nervous about the camp, because it was my first time away from my family. My family and I drove five hours north to get there. The drive was long and tiring, but it was worth it. The campgrounds were in a quiet rural town in upstate New York. We were surrounded by beautiful natural scenery. There were trees everywhere. My family stayed a while to see me settled in, then left. I felt a little bit homesick. But I was also very excited about this adventure. There were cabins for every age group, and for boys and girls. I was in the Mohawk cabin. The days flew by. Everyone did activities like swimming, fishing in the pond, music and drama, athletics, nature and more. I even caught a dark green turtle in the pond, but was scared to hold it because of its claws. We had a color war, and that was the best. My cabin's color was black. Before the games, we put black paint all over our bodies. Everyone in the camp went to the field, where we had a huge soccer tournament. I normally do not like sports, but I put everything into this particular soccer game. It was amazing! Another fun activity in camp was going to a dance! Everyone dressed up. I wore a beautiful, dark blue dress. And I had a date with a boy for the dance! He was very nice. It was a blast. My cabin-mates and I were always fooling around, jumping into the deep end of the pool, staying up late, and gossiping. The camp was a lot of fun, and probably like any other sleepaway camp in many ways. But what made it special was that every camper, and many of the camp counselors, had diabetes. There were kids getting insulin shots, kids on pumps and pods, and kids counting carbs. Everyone talked about their blood sugars, and diabetes related things. The words "insulin" and "bolus" were used often. This made me feel not alone anymore, and very happy, because I could relate to the girls in my cabin. On the first day, we had to test sugar after completing the swim test that determined who was allowed to swim in the deep end of the pool. Some of the girls in my cabin had crazy blood sugars. Some were crazy high, some were crazy low. One girl was even above 400! I always freaked out when my sugar went up close to 200. The crazy numbers that the girls in my cabin had weren't good, and should be treated right away. But at the same time, the crazy numbers helped me feel better about having diabetes, and helped me to worry less and not feel so upset about it, because those girls were doing fine and having fun. Camp showed me that I was not alone. Getting diabetes was a struggle, but it made me stronger. And I am so happy that I went to that camp, because I have remained connected with my cabin-mates through social media, and plan to stay in touch with them. We get to talk about how the diabetes devices that we are using are working out-there is a LOT going on in diabetes technology! And we also share when our sugar levels are super low or super high, and how we dealt with it. It is so good to have a group of people my age who can understand what I am going through!

Diabetes made me realize something amazing. It helped me realize that you never know how strong you are, until you are put into a challenging situation. I never even thought about diabetes before I was diagnosed. And when I was diagnosed I thought that no good would come from it. But I really believe that I am a better person because of what I went through!

Chapter Six- Finding Passion(s)

Throughout my life, I have had many passions. When I was younger, I loved gymnastics. I started taking gymnastics classes after school in fourth grade. I wasn't the most advanced gymnast, but it was really fun doing flips. Floor used to be my favorite event, and I always wanted to be more advanced. Once when I was in sixth grade, I asked my coach to do a skill called a back handspring. This is a jumping backward flip, using your hands to anchor you on the floor for the instant that you turn. At class I would do it with a coach spotting me. Every week, I wanted to do a back handspring on my own, with no spotting. Every week they said no, I was not ready. But then one day, I asked and the coach said ok. I jumped backwards on the tumble track, and landed badly on my hands. I knew something was wrong right away. Then I felt terrible, terrible pain. Yes.. I had broken my arm! I had to stop gymnastics for a while. But I begged my parents to send me back. After a year of begging they allowed me to go to another gymnastics place. I was scared, but I did get back to doing the back handspring. I learned to be more careful, but also to keep trying.

I stopped doing gymnastics in middle school when I became interested in other activities, like dance, art, and singing. Although I do not do it any more, I am glad that I did gymnastics because it was fun when I did it, and it also has helped me do well in other areas. For example, when I was in the *Willy Wonka* musical in eighth grade, I was an Oompa Loompa who did flips and splits on stage! I did not love that role, because it was such a small one, but doing the show was a start to loving theatre!

I have always been passionate about music. When I was about five or six years old I got an electronic keyboard for Christmas. I loved to experiment all day with different chords, sound effects, and keys. I started taking piano lessons at about eight years old. My piano teacher taught me how to read and count music. I got more advanced in piano, and started to compose my own music. I composed two songs that I have performed at recitals, called "Beautiful Day" and "Fallen Crystals." In third grade I started playing the violin in my elementary school's orchestra, and continued with orchestra and the violin in middle school, until I got to eighth grade, when I switched to choir for music class.

I began to love singing in middle school. I wasn't the best singer, though. In sixth grade, after I posted singing videos of myself on my Instagram, someone commented that I was not a good singer. That was pretty true at the time. Even now, there are still some people who think that I am a bad singer. As I wrote in the beginning, the pop singer Ariana Grande inspired me a lot at that time. I used to watch videos of her performing online, and I even went to her concert in 2015. I remember my mom trying to get me to practice the piano more instead of spending so much time listening to music on my iPhone. She told me that Ariana Grande was doing what was right for her, and making music, and that I should do what was right for me, and practice more so that I could get better at it, since I liked music so much. The truth was that I liked the piano, but I really wanted to be better at singing. When I watched Ariana Grande, I felt really happy and wanted to perform like her. I loved hearing her perform songs from her albums *My Everything* and *Dangerous Woman*. Ariana could belt really high notes, which I wanted to be able to do! Weekends in middle school were spent watching her, being inspired by her. I also practiced and practiced singing, and never gave up. Over time, I became good at belting and got a powerful voice. My voice was not like Ariana's voice, but I was ok with that. There is a song that I love to sing, called "Titanium" by Sia and David Guetta. It is a beautiful song with an amazing message. It is about not caring what others think, and not letting others get to you. That's exactly what I did with singing. When people made negative comments, I used that as motivation to practice more to become even better. And guess what? That practice paid off when I got into the high school's four-year vocal performing arts program, called PAVE Vocal.

When my mom mentioned PAVE for the first time it wasn't such a big deal to me, but I decided to audition in 8th grade. It was hard deciding on the right song for the audition. At first, I was going to sing "Because You Loved Me", by Celine Dion. I practiced in my living room at home. My mom thought that the way I sang it was beautiful, but I wanted to try something else. I thought that the song "Titanium" would be a better song. It had a great message, and it showed off my range. Over the next couple of months, I would practice "Titanium" at home, at music class, and at singing lessons. In March the audition day came. I made sure that I dressed my best for that day. I wore a pretty floral dress with tights and nice shoes. I even put on some makeup. The kids who were auditioning were supposed to leave during seventh period to get the bus to the high school. A bunch of kids and I left our class, and boarded the buses that left for the audition. Each bus has tons of students.

When the buses got to the high school, each PAVE subject (dance, acting, band, vocal, orchestra) went to a specific room. I went to the PAVE vocal room. The waiting process was difficult, and took a while. There were some high schoolers in the room who were enrolled in the PAVE program and were there to help us out with our auditions. I don't think that I was freaking out, but I was nervous. It was finally my turn. I walked into the room where everyone auditioning sang. There were two music teachers, and a piano to play the music. They asked a few questions, I handed them the sheet music, and then the music started. I sang *"You shout it out, but I can't hear a word you say…. I'm bullet proof, nothing to lose…"* I'm singing, I'm singing…. And SINGING! I sing the high part of the song, *"You shoot me down, but I won't fall…. I am Titanium!"* Oh my gosh! They didn't stop my audition too early! I actually got to the part where I could show off my range! Finally, after that part, one of the music teachers stopped me. Then, a note was played on piano, and I had to sing the note. I did well with this because I have perfect pitch (I know this because a music teacher had tested me when I was younger). I believe that I was told "good job" after the audition. Finally, my PAVE audition was over! When it was over for everyone, we all got on the buses to go back to the middle school. It was the end of the school day. I got into my mom's car after getting off the bus, and told her that my audition went fine. She was very proud of me. I kept wondering if I actually got in. Several days later, a letter arrived in the mail from the high school's PAVE department. It said that I had been accepted into the program! I was very happy about being accepted.

Getting into PAVE means that you do an extra course in your performing arts area every day in the morning before regular school starts, so I have to be at school almost an hour earlier than the kids who are not in PAVE. You also have to do a second performing arts class every day as an elective during the regular school day. In vocal arts PAVE, in one class you concentrate on solo performances and music theory, and the other class is about singing in a chorale, or chorus. Students get the opportunity to demonstrate what they learn several times during the school year at PAVE solo and choral concerts. A lot of people get anxiety from performing a solo, but not me! I sometimes do get a bit nervous, but I turn that nervous energy into excitement when I'm on stage! To be honest, PAVE class was only fun when I heard other people perform solos, or when I got to perform them. I did not like the chorus class as much. With chorus, since I was singing in a group I really did not get a chance to express myself, and I had no say in song choice. Music theory was difficult at first because the teacher's style was completely different to my piano teacher's. Also, no one talked to me for most of my first year of PAVE, so it was disappointing socially. I talked to the kids in PAVE about it on a group chat, but they read the message and didn't say anything. Later, I did make friends in PAVE, but learned that I needed to stop letting my past bother me and to talk more to people in person instead of online.

I have had great experiences because of PAVE. None of this would have happened if I had given up on singing. I started to look into other styles of music, such as musical theatre. I began to love musical theatre songs, because of the combination of singing and acting in them. I feel like singing musical theatre is cooler, because musical theatre music is more dramatic than pop and other genres. In many musical theatre songs, the character who is singing the song is passionate about what they want in life, or is singing about the emotions that they feel. The first musical theatre song that I fell in love with was "Defying Gravity" from the musical *Wicked!* I had trouble (and still do!) singing the high notes in that song. I think that now I do a much better job with it. "Defying Gravity" is a really empowering song. To me, it's all about rising above people who tell me what I cannot do. It is all about having self-confidence. I am not perfect at the song, but I love it. After that, I began to sing more musical theatre songs since they were more dramatic and better suited my belting style than other musical genres. My journey to PAVE taught me a huge lesson...work hard at something you want to be better at because.... you never know.

For my fifteenth birthday, I saw *Frozen* on Broadway, and it was amazing! At first I thought it may not be the best show for me because the movie is for little kids. I was wrong. And anyway, it was my all-time favorite movie when I was little. My brother and I had front row seats. Being in the front row was a great experience, because I got to see all of the special effects close up, like the ice queen's power. The singing and the acting from the entire cast was amazing. Afterwards, I waited at the stage door, along with some other fans, for the actors and actresses to come out. I told them how well they did, and they autographed my playbill. Moments like these make me realize how much I love to live within driving distance of New York City, and also how much I love the excitement of a show being acted out on a live stage.

Being in musicals is a great opportunity to do both singing and acting, and even if I don't get a good part, it is still a great experience, because I can learn many new things. I have been in a few musicals so far. At first, when I auditioned for shows and either got a bad part, or no part at all, I thought that the show directors saw nothing in me. But then I auditioned for the *25th Annual Putnam County Spelling Bee* show, and got a good part, with a singing solo, and a lot of lines. I played a speller named Leaf Coneybear. Even though I played a boy character, I really liked the role. Leaf was a very silly, crazy, and goofy role to play. I got to sing a song called "I'm Not That Smart", which I can sometimes relate to. There was a part in that song where I could be very silly and dance. It was fun! It was my first time with a bigger role, and at times I thought I wouldn't be able to play the part, but I was wrong! I didn't mess up on stage, and nothing went wrong. I learned not to doubt myself, and to look for big challenges. There were times when I knew that I was not as good as others when I tried out for parts, and

I am glad I did not quit, but instead worked on my singing and acting, and went to more auditions. Performing, singing and acting, is like my therapy. When I am on stage, I feel like I can express myself, which helps me feel in control. It is an amazing thing for me to get into character, because I can put my own spin on things. It is a lot of fun! I think that it is important for everyone to find their own passion in life. So many opportunities can come from doing something that you love, and that you are willing to work hard for! I think that the best advice for finding something you are passionate about is to experiment and try new things, because you never know what you'll like and the opportunities you might have. If you are in middle or high school, and your school has after-school clubs in sports, art, music, technology whatever....sign up even if you are not sure you want to! Because you never know.

I would honestly love to be on Broadway someday, because of one of my other inspirations in performing..... Idina Menzel.

In my freshman year of high school, I became a huge fan of hers. (I even met her twice quickly when she was leaving a play she was in!) I admired her amazing voice, her stage presence, and her ability to bring her characters to life. Even now, I love how she often plays misunderstood characters in her shows. She was the voice of Elsa in the movie *Frozen*, and was the first green witch in the musical *Wicked*. They are both roles of women who were considered to be evil only because other people did not understand who they really were. I relate to her because my experiences often make me feel misunderstood. Idina Menzel is my favorite actress because she shows that it's okay to be different. She helps me see myself in a better way. This is silly, but I would love to sing with Idina on stage at one of her concerts, or meet her again in a more meaningful way. I would honestly tell her so much, and how important she is to me. I don't know her personally, but she is one person that I fangirl over. I love theatre more because of her. I hope to continue with the performing arts, and take on bigger challenges, maybe even Broadway.

Chapter Seven -
Making Connections

Even though I have trouble in social situations, I still have good friends. The way I made all of my friends is by having a common interest. For example, when I was in fourth grade I met a very caring, sweet girl who is still one of my very special friends today. I will call her Ella. We met flipping on the bars in gymnastics class. She lived in another town, and therefore was in another school district. She asked me if I wanted to be best friends and I said yes of course. We don't do gymnastics anymore, but gymnastics is one thing that we had in common. Ella and I would always talk about our favorite events in gymnastics, and what skills we could do, and do flips together. I feel like even if she didn't ask me to be friends, we would have still been friends. We have a lot of other things in common. For example, we both love Ariana Grande! I don't see Ella very often, but it's lovely when we FaceTime and get to hang out. One of my favorite memories with her was going to her 11th birthday party… which was at a candy store in New York City! We drove to the city in a huge, black fancy limousine, with lots of music playing. The place shimmered colorfully with jars filled with different kinds of candies like peach rings, gummy sharks, and chocolate, and the party had lots of music and dancing and was very cute. I felt a little left out by the other girls at the party… but it was such a great experience! Ella is an amazing friend and she is always there for me. She always comes to my home for Halloween, and to my birthday parties.

I've also become friends with a set of twins, who I'll call B and K, from being in a school play. I don't see B and K a lot since they are in a lower grade and still in middle school, but we text often through Snapchat. I started talking to them during the *Willy Wonka* show rehearsals in middle school. We were all in the play together, and we would often rant about how annoying play practice was. Even though those conversations were kind of negative, it was a common experience that we had. There are also other friends that I've met from having classes together, by working in groups and talking about teachers. I think that the best way to make friends is to share something, because common interests can bring people together. I really love all my friends and hanging out with them. Now I sort of like that I'm not in a friend group, but instead have friends from my various experiences. Groups can be a little bit controlling, and it is good to have friends from different activities, who you can hang out with at different times.

Although social situations are difficult, I have learned to be better at making conversation. I used to jump into conversations when I was little, which isn't the best idea. I am quieter now and I usually do not start conversations first if I don't know people too well. I just wait to see how the conversation goes.

I also realized that because I felt awkward when I was with people in real life, I used texting and social media to over-share and I said too much online, especially about my feelings of not being liked. It is easy to say exactly what you feel when the person that you are communicating with is not in front of you. Now I am more careful about what I text and post.

I have craved friendship relationships because I've never had one that is as close as I would like. It hurts when I believe that a person is close to me, but they don't see me the same way. I do not like it when I ask a person to hang out, and they say that they are busy but they somehow make plans with other friends. I know now that in the past I tried too hard to make friendships happen, by reaching out too many times to the other person, and by over-sharing my feelings. I realize now that good friendships take time.

I still have a lot to learn about being social. But, even though I do go overboard sometimes, I believe I am a good friend. I am kind, friendly, and loving. I will always try to help my friends out no matter what, and I'm very accepting of others. I think that I can also have a very fun personality! At school (and outside of school) it sometimes feels like some of my friends would rather hang with "popular" kids, who are sometimes not the nicest people. Other than that, I am super happy about my friendships. No matter what my friends have said about me, I love each and every one of them. If someone doesn't want to be my friend, it is very hard to let them go. I remind myself about the good friends that I already have. Even though I have autism, I can still connect with other people. I have learned how to be better at using social media, and I have made a lot of great friends!

Chapter Eight - Accepting Me

To be honest, I am not the most confident person, and I have many insecurities. I am not even close to being perfect. But I have learned to accept some things about myself. For example, I have learned to accept my sensitivity. Ever since I was a little girl, I cried when my feelings were hurt, and they were hurt a lot. I'm not sure if being that emotional has anything to do with autism. I have heard that people with autism are not emotional, but it is the opposite for me. I feel like I got a bit too sensitive over the years, because of not being accepted by other kids, being bullied, and being left out. It sometimes felt like the world was beating me down. When I got older, my friends would get annoyed at me for how I reacted, and that made me upset. One of my friends told me that I was too emotional and that I over-reacted over everything. I know that it is important to have a thick skin at times, but being emotional is just a part of me, and I've learned to accept it. One day in my high school freshman year, after I was diagnosed with diabetes, I was in Spanish class. I asked my teacher to use the bathroom, but she said no. She said that we were supposed to use the bathroom between class periods, not during them. I got up to try to tell her that I had a medical reason (diabetes made me go a lot sometimes), and I really needed to go, but she shook her head. So I had to say it out loud - in front of the entire class! Some kids laughed. Eventually I was able to use the bathroom, but I could tell when I came back that she was mad. I was so upset. That was my last class for the day, and afterwards I headed to an afterschool club called Yes Girls (not its real name). Yes Girls is a club that helps girls become more confident and empowered through different activities that build confidence and leadership skills. I was pretty new to the club (a school counselor had suggested it to me) and I did not know anyone very well. The girls in that club were so confident, and always seemed happy. They were vocal, and always spoke about being strong and taking care of yourself and what they believed in. Female empowerment is important to me. I liked being in the club, but I also felt intimidated when I went there. I was not as confident as the other girls. I felt like Yes Girls was the right club for me, because I say what is on my mind a lot, and I don't keep much to myself. But they were more confident. I felt that they were better than me. That day, after the Spanish teacher embarrassed me, I sat there trying to listen to what the club director was saying, but I kept thinking about what the teacher did, and I started to cry. Some of the other girls saw me and asked me what the matter was, and I shared what had happened with them. To be honest, I think that maybe I cried partly because I wanted to talk about what happened. The girls said that I should not have let the teacher talk to me like that. They said that I should have stood up to her and walked out of the class instead of waiting for her to give permission, if I really needed to go. And also, they said that I was too soft and that as women we should be tough and not allow other people to make us cry. I knew that they were trying to help, but they made me feel even worse! They were telling me that I was not like them, that I was different. I was weak and could not stand up for myself. I was so tired of feeling different from everyone else. That was such a bad day. But over the next few days, I felt better. I realized that deep down I really do believe my favorite Dr. Seuss quote: "Today You are You, that is Truer than True. There is no one alive who is You-er than You." I don't want to walk out on a teacher, that's not me. I don't have to be loud to get my ideas across to other people, I can do it in my own way. Maybe sometimes I do need to speak up sooner, and I need to cry less when things go wrong, but I'm still learning, and I can do that without pretending to be someone else.

I have also become comfortable with being different in the way that I dress. In sixth grade, kids laughed at me for liking brightly colored Justice brand clothes. More recently, in 9th grade, I posted a message on Snapchat asking people to swipe up on Sarahah. Sarahah is an "honesty app" that can be accessed in Snapchat where people can get anonymous feedback about themselves from other people. One person commented that I dressed like I was still in 5th grade. I wouldn't say that I dress like a little kid, but I'm not a huge fan of most of the clothing that the girls wear in my school. I like the ripped jeans, but some of the other teen clothing is not my style. Many high school girls wear crop tops, sweatpants, and dark colors, but I would rather wear skirts, dresses, and bright colors most days. I have gotten teased and made fun of for the way I dressed, but learned to accept my different style. If I tried to copy everyone and wear dark colors all the time, I wouldn't be myself. Bright colors, skirts, and dresses are what I like to wear, and wearing them is what makes me unique. There are some trends that I follow and like, but I wouldn't change my entire style just to fit in and become popular. I would rather be me! I do want to fit in sometimes, but not at the expense of losing who I am!

I am also learning to accept bad things that happen in my life that I have no control over, like…diabetes. Having diabetes can be upsetting at times. I get very anxious when my blood sugar gets high. When I get anxious, it is so distracting and so difficult to focus on what I need to do, like my school-work. What helps me is to learn as much as I can about the disease, and to do what I need to in terms of healthy eating and exercise to keep those blood sugar numbers under control and in the right range. I eat differently from before the diagnosis. I don't eat candy and high sugar foods daily any more. I still enjoy them, but just space them out, and I look forward to them as treats. I try to eat more proteins and good fats along with carbs because that is supposed to slow down the rate at which carbohydrates are broken down into glucose after eating, which prevents blood sugar spikes. I also now run for exercise, because it helps bring down high blood sugar levels, but also because it helps me feel less stressed. My blood sugar numbers are fine most of the time, but there have been a few times when I do all of the things I am supposed to do, but my numbers are above or below the acceptable range and I have no idea why. I am trying to "listen" to my body to learn signs for when this starts happening so I can take care of it as soon as possible. Signs include headaches and feeling light headed. When I am out of my acceptable blood sugar range, I also remember that my camp counselor at the diabetes sleepaway camp said that sometimes factors that are beyond our control (like hormones) can make it get out of range, and I shouldn't worry too much when it happens.

Chapter Nine – Overcoming

Autism has had a big impact on my life. As you can see, I've had a lot of bad social experiences and have been left out because of it. Often, I felt that kids who were around me did not understand me. I sometimes wished that I was normal, but I've been told that there is no normal, and that everyone is unique. Autism is a part of me. Having autism could also mean that I have a unique way of thinking. Who knows, maybe autism is the reason for my interest in science related things. Although I knew and read about autism since I was about seven years old (my mom told me about it when I asked about why I was different), the first time that it really mattered to me was when I took a state test in fourth grade. My teacher circled "has a disability" on a form that was in front of me. That was the very first time that I felt ashamed about having autism. It was not a good feeling. But I'm happy that I also overcame many challenges that I met on my autism journey. For example, I used to go to group speech therapy in elementary school. I always wondered why I went to speech, because my talking was fine. I know that when I was little, in preschool, I used to do this thing where I always repeated a question that someone asked me before answering it. So if a teacher asked me "Where is the book?" I would answer: "Where is the book? The book is on the table!" I am pretty sure that I stopped speaking that way by the time I got to kindergarten, but they still made me do speech therapy. There, I met with the therapist and a couple of other kids, and practiced things like spelling words, and sentences, and conversations. From kindergarten to third grade I was okay with going. In fourth and fifth grade I dreaded going to speech, because it made me feel abnormal. On top of that, I felt that I didn't need the extra help. So I worked really hard to show the therapist my abilities. One day, she said that I didn't need speech therapy anymore. I felt so relieved. That was one challenge I overcame, and I'm still working to overcome even more. Having autism isn't good or bad; it's a difference, which might have caused me painful social experiences and challenges, but it is part of what makes me unique. Everyone has obstacles, and autism has produced some of mine. The obstacles we go through make us, us!

Overcoming academic obstacles was a major part of my first year of high school. Schoolwork was a challenge in ninth grade. It did not help that because I got diagnosed with type 1 diabetes, I missed several days of school, both when I was in the hospital and when I got fitted with the Omnipod pump device. But even before the diabetes drama happened, I had difficulty with my classwork. A big reason for this is that it was hard for me to keep track of school paperwork. There was so much of it! Notes from class, homework worksheets, quizzes…and for five main subjects – math, bio, global history, Spanish, English - plus the performing arts classes. Oh, plus a science research class that I took as an elective. I am not sure how, but many times after I'd lost my notes from global history, I would find them weeks later in my math binder. Usually I would find it long after I had taken the global history test for the topic those notes covered. This was just one reason why I did not do very well in global history tests.

Another reason was that global history required SO MUCH READING! It is supposed to tell a story -the story of human-kind over the years, but I didn't know what I was supposed to imagine, and I had trouble keeping the events straight, which made me get super stressed. I think that global history got a bit better as the year went on, but it was still difficult. I tried really hard to read the text like a story, and to imagine the set of events happening. But it did not work - I felt like I needed to memorize everything, and it was usually too much information to do that, especially since I usually started studying the day before the test, which did not give me a lot of time!

In addition, focusing in class took a lot of energy. In class, I zoned out a lot. In math I would start off the class paying attention, but then my thoughts would begin to distract me.

I would be hungry in class, or tired, or I'd think about what I was going to do over the summer. I usually didn't become aware that I was distracted until much later in the class, and by the time I snapped back to reality the teacher was way ahead and it was difficult to follow what he was doing.

I knew that zoning out was a problem for me, so I tried hard to focus. But concentrating on staying focused took a ton of energy, and made me tired. Also, because I was in the performing arts program, I had to get to school an hour earlier than the regular start of school, so I usually started the day tired. I fell asleep in class quite a few times. Once I fell asleep in my English class, and my teacher wrote me a note, asking nicely if I was getting enough sleep. That was so embarrassing!

So, ninth grade has been tough for me! I used to have an A -minus average in middle school, but in my first year of high school, all my subjects pretty much dropped by a letter grade. But it was not all bad. I learned that I really enjoyed biology. Maybe I would like a career in that field. Finding out that I had type 1 diabetes, a genetic disease, and also having autism, which is a neurological disorder, makes me curious about how the human body works. I did well on my bio final, and did ok in my other classes. By the end of the school year, I learned how to study better: I paid more attention to test dates and gave myself more time to study, and I went to extra help after school more. I tried and am still trying to figure out my learning style. It was hard for me to listen to words without seeing them on paper, so I knew I was not an auditory learner. I learned best when I got to complete hands-on activities that were about the subject matter I was trying to master. This is why the only time I enjoyed English class was when we did plays. I understood Shakespeare so much better when I got to act it out. I guess this is also why I liked science labs. Looking back, I learned that I was smarter that I thought I was at the beginning of the school year, and I could handle more than I thought I would be able to handle. I plan to become more organized and to study smarter for 10th grade (but I am still figuring out what that means!)

My love for theatre motivates me to overcome a challenge that I have dealt with since I was a little kid. Like many other people on the autism spectrum, I find it uncomfortable to make eye contact with another person for a long period of time. I can't really explain it, but it doesn't feel good. When I am acting, I often have dialogues with other characters, where I need to be looking at them. When this happens, I usually get an urge to look away, which can affect my performance. I have been practicing staring into the eyes of family and friends, so that I can be comfortable with it at show rehearsals, and of course for performances! I am not there yet but I will be!

I am also getting better at communicating with people and standing up for myself. I was in a production of *Footloose!* at a musical theatre studio a few weeks after I returned from sleepaway camp the summer after ninth grade. In it, I played the part of a high school kid who was a friend of one of the main characters. I got to do some solo singing parts, which was fun. But I had a bit of trouble with learning the lines for the parts that did not involve singing. I kept messing up some of the words. The girl who had the lead role got mad at me for messing up. She kept freaking out, saying that the show had to be perfect. She would move out of her spot to tell me what I should do and what I was not doing correctly. Eventually, I told her that I wanted to talk to her privately. I told her in private that she was not the show's director, and that it was not her job to tell me what to do. I asked her not to do it again. The director found out about the situation and had a talk with the girl, who got upset and left early that day. But the director told me that I had done the right thing. That girl and I were fine afterwards. I stopped forgetting my lines during rehearsal and we all got along. The show went off and it was great. I realized then that I had the confidence to stand up for myself and to speak up when one of my peers is going overboard trying to "teach" me something.

That's very different to the person that I was a year earlier.

PART THREE:
BUILDING MY
RAINBOW

Chapter Ten - Facing my Future

So, that is pretty much my story, from my early years to now. I have learned so much! But this isn't the end. Life keeps going on, and I have to plan for the future! First, I hope to be successful for the rest of high school, college, and beyond. I will do so by working hard in tenth, eleventh and twelfth grade. In school, I will try my absolute hardest to pay attention, and start working hard from the start of the school year. It is important to make good grades in high school, because grades start counting for college. Second, I want to do something amazing when I grow up. I am sure that even then I would love to audition and perform for a Broadway show. I would like to play a strong female role with a lot of belt singing, and great acting. Even if I don't get the "top" role in the most popular Broadway show, I would still be okay. It will be hard, but I'm willing to work for my dreams!

I love performing, but I am also interested in working in science. I am learning about careers in biology because this may be what I want to do after college. Science is the answer to how the world really works. In biology class, I am so interested in learning how body cells function and how organs work together. It would be very cool to find new ways for managing diabetes, like new ways to get insulin, and new technologies! In fact, it would be great to investigate ways to improve the health and quality of life for people with all types of diseases.

I would also love to help children with autism. Since I was about 8 or 9 years old, I have been part of a research study at a center for autism research at a major university. Every few years, I go there and a group of researchers ask me a ton of questions about my social life and how I am doing in school. They also have me fill out lots of interview sheet forms. My mom also comes and they interview her separately too. When I was younger, they gave me toys to play with and watched how I played with them. They did all this to learn more about how I and all the other research subjects who have autism are developing, and also to find out how to help kids like me in the future. I might be interested in doing research like this that helps the world to learn more about the disorder. I did an elective in 9th grade called science research, where we read articles from various medical and science journals and I got to see examples of the research process. Even though I was really disorganized in that class and lost some of the papers that I should have read, I found that class to be really interesting, and it made me think that maybe I would like to do some of the work that the researchers who interviewed me at the autism research center are doing.

I have other goals that do not have to wait until I finish high school, and I am looking forward to focusing on them. I hope that I can use my story to help spread awareness about the hurt experienced by kids when they are excluded and bullied. So many children and teens, with or without diagnosed social disorders like autism, feel left out of their school community. Helping other kids know that they can help stop the pain of another person by simple actions of inclusion is important, because most kids are good and want to help, but often they just don't know that a problem exists. Beyond spreading awareness, I want to find a way to help kids who struggle with making friends to connect socially. It would be so great to help them be part of something bigger than themselves, feel included and make new friends. When kids feel connected, they feel better about themselves and do better at life!

I hope this book has inspired someone. I had a lot of emotions writing about my story. I felt passionate writing about doing what I loved, which is performing. I felt very hopeful writing about what I want to do in the future. I felt heartbroken and depressed writing about all my bad memories of kids from elementary school rejecting me and not liking me. My social history may not be the best, and at times my life felt really cloudy. But I found out so much by looking through those clouds. I've learned that I can memorize more lines than I thought I could. I learned to accept some aspects of myself, and realize that I'm one of a kind. I am very thankful to God for all of my opportunities in life. All of these positives are the colors of my rainbow. I got these colors by living through my experiences, including bad ones, and learning from them. Good can come out of bad. In the middle of a stressful middle school experience, I found my passion for singing, then got into the PAVE vocal 4-year high school program that I love. From diabetes, I got stronger, braver and learned more about being independent. From being rejected from the school play... I got to be in another very cool show! From having a tough freshman year, I learned more about my learning style and what I need to do to be better in class. I am putting all of these colors together to build a rainbow that is pointing me in the direction of my future. I know that as time goes on, I will continue to have more good and bad experiences, I will keep adding more new colors, and my rainbow will shine stronger and brighter. And I hope that somehow this book can help someone else who is experiencing a cloudy day to search for their own colors and build their own, fabulous rainbow!

The End
(well, almost.. please turn page!)

Afterword

Here are some of my favorite showtune songs. If you like, make a playlist and listen to my rainbow!

Song: *Defying Gravity*
Show: *Wicked*
Defying Gravity is about overcoming challenges, following your dreams, and being confident in yourself. Very empowering.
Favorite Lyric: *"As someone told me lately..Everyone deserves the chance to fly"*

Song: *This Is Me*
Show: *The Greatest Showman*
This song is all about self-acceptance!!!!!!!
Favorite Lyric: *"I am brave, I am bruised, I am who I'm meant to be, this is me"*

Song: *I Know Where I've Been*
Show: *Hairspray*
This song is about fighting for justice and equality. But to me, it is also about never

giving up on something you are passionate about, or never giving up on something you believe in.

Favorite Lyric: *"There's a road, we've been traveling. Lost so many, on the way. But the riches will be plenty..Worth the price, the price we had to pay"*

Song: *Waiting For Life*
Show: *Once On This Island*
I love this song because it is about being excited and open to what life has to offer!

Favorite Lyric: *"I'm here in the field, With my feet on the ground, And my fate in the air, Waiting for life to begin!"*

Song: *Don't Rain On My Parade*
Show: *Funny Girl*
This song is about not caring about what others think, knowing that sometimes... listening to other's opinions is not helpful.... it's about not letting others.... "rain on your parade!" I love the message.

Favorite Lyric: *"Don't tell me not to live, Just sit and putter"*

Song: *My Shot*
Show: *Hamilton*
I love this song so much! I will never give away my "shot" in life!
Favorite Lyric: *"I am just like my country, I'm young scrappy and hungry, and I'm not throwing away my shot!"*

Song: *Let It Go*
Show: *Frozen*
I know that everyone is tired of hearing this song, but the message is so important! *Let It Go* is all about embracing what makes you different, and not trying to be exactly like everyone else. All about being confident!
Favorite Lyric: *"I'm never going back, the past is in the past!"*

Song: *Live Out Loud*
Show: *A Little Princess*
Favorite Lyric: *"Why do I have to hide what I'm feeling inside, I wanna live out loud!!"*

To hear more, visit
www.sociallyconnectedunicorn.com

CPSIA information can be obtained
at www.ICGtesting.com
Printed in the USA
BVHW030141131121
621519BV00020B/119

9 781644 385159